Penguin Functional

PAIR WORK

Activities for Effective Communication   *Student A*

Peter Watcyn-Jones

Penguin Books

Penguin Books Ltd, Harmondsworth, Middlesex, England
Penguin Books, 40 West 23rd Street, New York, New York 10010, U.S.A.
Penguin Books Australia Ltd, Ringwood, Victoria, Australia
Penguin Books Canada Ltd, 2801 John Street, Markham, Ontario, Canada L3R 1B4
Penguin Books (N.Z.) Ltd, 182–190 Wairau Road, Auckland 10, New Zealand

First published 1981
Reprinted 1982, 1984

Made and printed in Great Britain by
Butler & Tanner Ltd, Frome and London

ISBN 0 14 081 320 9
Pair Work Student B ISBN 0 14 081 321 7

Contents

Acknowledgements

The author and publishers wish to thank the following for the use of copyright material in this book: British Tourist Authority for p. 17; Courtaulds Limited for p. 37; Greater London Council Photograph Library for p. 35; Hastings Tourism and Recreation Department, Information Centre, Hastings for the adaptation of the stylized map on p. 53; Pilgrims Publications Canterbury and Carlos Maeztu for allowing us to base Unit 1 on 'From a Humanistic Education Workshop led by Howard Kirshenbaum' taken from the book *Recipe Book for Tired Teachers – No 1* under the title 'Dynamic Encounter'.

To the teacher

Pair Work forms part of the Penguin Functional English course and was written to give classes, working in pairs, further practice in the functions introduced in *Impact* and *Dialogues*. Unlike most courses, *Pair Work* consists of two books, one for Student A and the other for Student B. There are two basic reasons for this:

1 In most language situations there is always an element of the unexpected – of not knowing exactly what the person you are talking to is going to say, even though on some occasions you may have a general idea (e.g. when ordering food in a restaurant). Unfortunately, most books give little practice in this since all too often every student has access to the same material as everyone else in the class with the result that anything that is said is often predictable. This, in turn, gives the students a false sense of security, so that once the whole context or the set-piece is removed they often find difficulty in communicating outside the classroom. *Pair Work* tries to overcome this by making sure from the beginning that Student A does not have access to Student B's information, and vice versa. In this way students are forced to react with one another and to respond to the unexpected – which is, after all, an essential requirement for true communication.

2 Another important aspect of language learning which again is often neglected is training students to listen effectively. Whereas listening comprehension exercises are an attempt to overcome this problem they are, in most cases, fairly passive activities and all too often removed from reality. Instead, what we should be concentrating on is in students listening effectively to one another. Again, when all the information is available to everyone in the class such intensive listening is not necessary since the student can always read anything he or she does not understand. But by removing what the other speaker is going to say the student is immediately forced into a situation where he or she not only has to but wants to listen intensively in order to be able to talk to the other person – which is, after all, the situation he or she is going to be in when he or she leaves the comparative safety of the classroom.

Description of the material

Each book contains forty activities. These are arranged, where possible, into pairs of activities so that if Student A has one particular role or task in the first activity then he or she has Student B's role or task in the second, and vice versa. This gives both students practice in the same function but avoids the possibly boring alternative of simply changing parts and doing exactly the same activity again. Instead of this, the same function is practised again but the situation (or role) is changed. (See Note 1, page 7)

There are five main types of activities in the books:

1 Role-plays
These are activities in which students are given definite roles to play and are usually asked to assume a different name, background, age, etc. (See Note 2)

An example of a role-play is Activity 17 – Newspaper interviews.

2 Simulation exercises
These are activities in which students can play themselves but are given a definite task to do or are put in a specific situation and asked to make appropriate responses.

An example of a simulation exercise is Activity 8 – Asking for train information.

3 One-sided dialogues
These are activities in which students read a dialogue together but can only see their own part, which usually includes opportunities for the student to make his or her own responses.

An example of a one-sided dialogue is Activity 10 – At a restaurant.

4 Information-gap activities
These are activities in which students are asked to perform a task together; they fall into two types. In the first, one student has access to all the information and tries to impart it to his or her partner.

An example of this type is Activity 15 – Complete the drawing (1). In the second, both students are given access to half the information and by working together try to solve the whole.

An example of this type is Activity 13 – Fill in the missing information (1).

5 Discussion and conversation activities
These are activities designed to stimulate students to discuss a subject or subjects with their partner and usually take the form of a questionnaire. These activities are particularly useful when students are practising giving opinions and showing agreement or disagreement.

An example of a discussion or conversation activity is Activity 14 – Children and parents.

How to use the books

Since the activities have been written to give extra practice in certain functions they are best done as follow-up work since the books assume that the student has a basic mastery of the language needed to perform the various functions. Again, although specifically written to supplement *Impact* and *Dialogues* there is no reason why the books cannot be used with any other existing functionally based course at intermediate level or above.

A list of functions is given on page 8 with the number of the activity or activities which practise them. All the teacher has to do is decide which function needs practising and choose an appropriate activity from the ones given. Since, in some instances, more than one activity has been written to practise a particular function, repeated practice can be given without the students becoming bored. Since the level throughout the book is intermediate there is no need to take the activities in order if the needs of the class dictate otherwise. Indeed, it is not envisaged that the book should be worked through from beginning to end: the activities can, and should, be taken in any order depending on the needs of any particular class.

Teaching hints

1 Clear instructions are given for all the activities so that all the teacher has to do is ask the students to turn to a particular activity and let them read through the instructions. While the students do this, the teacher can go around the class checking that they have fully understood what they have to do before starting. When the students are ready they begin. It is better if all the pairs start working at the same time, rather than working one after the other.

2 Before starting, the room should be arranged in such a way that pairs face one another across a desk or table. This is to give them 'eye-contact' which makes communication a lot easier. Again, if possible, a bag or some sort of screen should be placed between them so that they cannot see one another's books.

3 Since the students will be working in pairs, the pairs should be changed as often as possible so that students get a chance to work with (and get to know) different people in the class.

4 Should the group be made up of an odd number of students, then the teacher may be forced into working with one of the students. If this is nearly always the case, the teacher should choose a different student to work with each time. However, if a teacher feels reluctant to join in there is no reason why one of the students couldn't act as a passive observer and sit and listen to one of the pairs – noting, if possible, any mistakes which are made and commenting afterwards on the pair's performance. The student could then exchange roles with one of the more confident students, so that at least one role is taken by every student in the class.

5 During an activity the teacher moves from pair to pair, as a passive observer, noting problems or mistakes which can be taken up with the whole group after the activity has finished. In fact, it is always a good idea to spend a few minutes discussing the activity afterwards.

6 It is a good idea occasionally after a group has done a particular activity to ask one of the pairs to carry out the activity while the rest of the group listen and comment on their performance.

7 The length of the activities varies from approximately five to twenty minutes although, if the group is a particularly imaginative one, some of them (especially the role-plays) could take longer. It is up to the teacher and group to decide whether to spend a whole lesson on the activities or else to make them a part of a normal lesson. (Perhaps a combination of these two is a good idea.)

8 Although Activities 1 and 2 give practice in asking and answering personal questions, the chief reason for putting them first in the book is that they are a useful way of breaking the ice when the group is a new one – although they are still useful when the group has been together for some time. However, if the group includes students who are sensitive about giving personal information about themselves, the teacher can tell them not to answer any question which they may not wish to answer; they can simply say they cannot think of anything in reply to these questions.

9 Not all activities are appropriate for all classes. Any which are not can simply be omitted (for example, Activity 14 may not be acceptable in all cultures).

Notes

1 Of course, if the teacher and group would like to repeat activities, then there is no reason why students couldn't change books and do them again. This can be done at a later date.

2 For more detailed notes on role-play as well as further examples, see another book by Peter Watcyn-Jones, *Act English* (also published by Penguin Books Ltd).

Guide to functions practised

Function	Number of activity
Asking and answering personal questions	1, 2
Asking and answering questions about likes and dislikes	3
Asking and answering questions about future plans	4, 13
Asking about and stating wants and needs	5, 6, 10, 11, 12, 31, 32
Giving advice	7 (dialogue 1)
Passing on and reacting to a piece of news	7 (dialogue 2)
Apologies and excuses	7 (dialogues 3, 4), 26 (situations 1, 2)
Giving opinions/agreeing and disagreeing with an opinion	14, 19
Giving and receiving instructions	15, 16, 24, 25
Asking for and giving information	8, 9, (13), 33, 34, 37
Asking and answering questions	17, 18, 20, 21, 27, 29, 35, 38
Asking for and making suggestions	22
Socializing	26 (situation 3), 28, 39
Asking for and giving directions	23
Asking for help	26 (situation 4)
Talking about degrees of certainty/uncertainty	30
Inviting and making arrangements	36
Two 'sort it out' activities	39, 40

Getting to know one another

Read the sentences below and write down your answers on the following page.

Look at the top left-hand corner of the next page:

Next to number 1, write down the year when you first went abroad.

Next to number 2, write down the name of the most beautiful place you have ever visited.

Next to number 3, write down what you would be if you could choose any job in the world.

In the circle under number 3, write down the first name of your best friend.

Look at the bottom right-hand corner:

Next to number 4, write down the first name (surname if you don't know it) of the teacher at school you hated most.

Next to number 5, write down something that frightens you.

Next to number 6, write down the first name of the person you admire most (living or dead).

In the circle above number 4, write down the name of the country you would most like to visit.

Look at the top right-hand corner:

In the rectangle, write down the year when you were happiest.

In the circle underneath, write down what you consider to be the ideal number of children in a family.

Look at the bottom left-hand corner:

In the rectangle, write down the name of the town or village where you were born.

In the circle above, write down the number of people in your family, including yourself (people living at home).

Look at the large rectangle in the middle of the page:

Write your first name in the rectangle in LARGE LETTERS.

In the blank spaces around it write down three things you enjoy doing.

When you have finished, change books with Student B. Look at what he or she has written and ask him or her as many questions as you can about it, e.g. What does this date here mean? Who is this person? etc. Try to get him or her to talk as much as possible about each thing. (Of course, you will also be expected to talk about what you have written!)

1 _____

2 _____

3 _____

4 _____

5 _____

6 _____

Questionnaire:
what sort of person are you?

Read through the sentences below, then put a circle around the number which most closely coincides with the way you usually behave. Before starting, look at the Key.

		KEY
I find it easy to get out of bed in the mornings.	I 2 3 4 5	1 Yes, always
I watch at least one T.V. programme or listen to at least one radio programme in the evenings.	I 2 3 4 5	2 Yes, usually 3 Well, it depends
I feel nervous when meeting new people.	I 2 3 4 5	4 No, not usually
I am good with money.	I 2 3 4 5	5 No, never
I feel bored when I am alone.	I 2 3 4 5	
I would rather be with members of the opposite sex than with members of my own sex.	I 2 3 4 5	
I try to keep up with the latest world news.	I 2 3 4 5	
I get annoyed if people are late.	I 2 3 4 5	
I prefer going out at weekends to staying at home.	I 2 3 4 5	
I think things over carefully before making a decision.	I 2 3 4 5	
I try to make at least one or two new friends every year.	I 2 3 4 5	
I go abroad in the summer.	I 2 3 4 5	
I remember people's names when I am introduced to them.	I 2 3 4 5	
I plan for the future.	I 2 3 4 5	
I find it easy to learn English.	I 2 3 4 5	

When you have finished, compare your answers with Student B. Try to discuss each point – giving reasons why you do or don't do something.

3 Market research — television or radio programmes

You work for a Market Research Bureau. You are doing research into the types of television or radio programmes people watch or listen to. You stop people in the street to ask them questions and write down their answers in pencil on the sheet below. Student B is a passer-by.

MARKET RESEARCH   TELEVISION/RADIO QUESTIONNAIRE

1 How many hours a week do you spend watching television or listening to the radio?

	less than 5 hours
	5–10 hours
	10–15 hours
	15–20 hours
	more than 20 hours

2 What sort of programmes do you like watching or listening to?

3 Are there any sorts of programmes you don't like?

Like	Dislike	
		the news
		films or discussion programmes
		quiz shows
		pop music programmes
		comedy programmes
		documentaries
		classical music programmes
		serials
		plays
		detective series
		chat shows
		children's programmes
		variety shows
		sports programmes
		(others)....................

4   What is your favourite programme?

5   Are there any sorts of programmes
    you would like   (a) more of?   ....

                                       ....

                        (b) less of?   ....

                                       ....

You can begin like this:

Excuse me, can I ask you some questions about television/radio?

And finish:

Thank you very much for answering my questions.

4   Holiday survey

You are going on a charter holiday with your wife/husband and two children to the West Indies in June. You are going for two weeks and are staying at the Ravioli Hotel. You hope to do a lot of sightseeing and are planning to visit a number of islands. You are also looking forward to the sunshine and plan to go swimming every day. You have been to the West Indies several times and think this is one of the best places to go for a holiday. You are flying from Heathrow.

Student B is doing a survey on how people spend their summer holidays and is going to interview you about your holiday plans. Answer his/her questions.

Booking a room at a hotel (1)

★★**Longhouse** Royal Parade, BN22 7AH
☎031451 Plan **11**
Three-storey Victorian terrace, with green-roofed sun terrace and modern entrance.
Uninterrupted views of sea.

★★**Surrey** Cornfield Terrace (Centre) ☎927681
Telex no 963561 Plan **22**
Three-storey, steep-roofed building of brick and stone, with modern entrance.

★**Highland** Plan **17** Converted Victorian terrace house overlooking sea.

You are on holiday in England with your wife/husband. You are staying in London at present but would like to visit Southbourne for a few days. You decide to phone up the Surrey Hotel (above) and make a reservation.

You want to stay for three nights and would like a double room with bath, overlooking the sea, if possible. You also need a room on the ground floor or first floor because your wife has difficulty in climbing stairs (should the lift be out of order).

You will be arriving by train tomorrow and want to know how far the hotel is from the station.

Student B is the hotel receptionist.

You can begin like this:

Good (*morning*). My name's (*David Brown*). I'd like to book a room at your hotel for three nights.

Booking a room at a hotel (2)

THE MONARCH HOTEL
Seafront Parade
Dackton
Tel: (0873) 921215

* Overlooks the beach
* 100 bedrooms, most with private bathroom
* Central heating and air-conditioning throughout
* 2 lifts to all floors
* Large bars and restaurants
* Nightly entertainment
* Night porter
* 3 T.V. lounges
* Private car park
* 5 mins from Dolphinarium

CHARGES PER NIGHT – BED AND BREAKFAST

Single room	£18.50
Single room with bath	£20.00
Twin/double room	£24.50
Twin/double room with bath	£26.00
Extra bed in room	£5.00
T.V. in same room	£1.00

You are a receptionist at the Monarch Hotel in Dackton. Student B phones up to make a reservation.

Before starting, have a pen or pencil ready to write down all the necessary information. Make sure you get the following:

1 The person's name (you may have to ask him/her to spell it).
2 The type of room required (e.g. single, double, etc.).
3 The day/date of arrival.
4 Length of stay.

You can also include other details about the hotel – e.g. if it has a restaurant, entertainment, is near the sea, etc.

Here is a form you can use when writing down the necessary information:

Name: ....

Accommodation: ....

Date of arrival: ....

Length of stay: ....

Other details: ....

You can begin like this:

Good (*morning*). Monarch Hotel.

7   Carrying on a conversation

Below are the opening words of four dialogues. Working with Student B, try to make the conversation go on for as long as possible. Before starting, think for a few minutes about what it might be possible to say. (But do *not* discuss the dialogue with Student B!) When you are both ready, begin the conversation.

Dialogue 1
You play the part of A. Student B plays the part of B.

> A: You look upset,......(*say person's name*).
>   What's wrong?
> B: Oh, it's just that......(*carry on the conversation*).

Dialogue 2
You play the part of B. Student B plays the part of A.

> A: It's a pity about John, isn't it?
> B: John? What do you mean?
> A: Well, haven't you heard?
> B: Heard what?
> A: ...... (*carry on the conversation*).

Dialogue 3
You play the part of A. Student B plays the part of B.

> A: 978574.
> B: Hello. Is that...... (*say person's name*)?
> A: Yes.
> B: It's...... (*say your name*). Where on earth were you last night?
> A: Last night?...... (*carry on the conversation*).

Dialogue 4
You play the part of B. Student B plays the part of A.

> A: Excuse me, is that your dog over there?
> B: Yes, that's right.
> A: Well, it's just bitten my friend!
> B: ...... (*carry on the conversation*).

Asking for train information 8

You are at present living and working in Paris. Your cousin is getting married in Madrid on Saturday. You phone up the Central Station to find out the times of the trains to and from Madrid.

The wedding is at 11.15 in the morning. You wish to arrive in Madrid either on Friday evening or early Saturday morning (booking a sleeper, if necessary). You must be back in Paris in time for a meeting at 12.30 on Monday.

Student B is a clerk at the Central Station.

Before starting, have a pen ready to make a note of the following:

> Time/day of departure from Paris ....
>
> Time/day of arrival in Madrid ....
>
> Time/day of departure from Madrid....................................
>
> Time/day of arrival in Paris ....

You can begin like this:

> Good (*morning*). I'd like some information about trains from Paris to Madrid.

9   Asking for boat information

You are a clerk for the Fjord Line which runs boats between England (Felixstowe) and Sweden (Gothenburg). Student B phones you up for some information about boats to Gothenburg. Answer his/her inquiries with the help of the time-table and fare lists.

FELIXSTOWE–GOTHENBURG   Time-table   July

FELIXSTOWE			GOTHENBURG		
Day	Date	Time	Day	Date	Time
Mon	2	20.30	Tue	3	20.30
Thu	5	13.30	Fri	6	13.00
Fri	6	13.00	Sat	7	13.00
Sun	8	18.00	Mon	9	17.30
Mon	9	20.30	Tue	10	20.30
Thu	12	13.30	Fri	13	13.00
Fri	13	13.00	Sat	14	13.00
Sun	15	18.00	Mon	16	17.30

FELIXSTOWE–GOTHENBURG   Passenger fares – one way (not including accommodation)

Sailing period	From Felixstowe	Adults	Children
25 April–1 October	Monday	£35	£18
	Thursday, Friday, Sunday	£40	£20

FELIXSTOWE–GOTHENBURG	Accommodation charges (25 April–1 October)	
Type of berth		Cost per person, one way
4 berth economy cabin	3 persons in cabin	£3.50
	2 persons in cabin	£7.00
4 berth inside de-luxe cabin	4 persons in cabin	£7.00
	3 persons in cabin	£10.50
4 berth outside de-luxe cabin	4 persons in cabin	£10.50
	3 persons in cabin	£14.00
Twin bunk de-luxe cabin	2 persons in cabin	£17.50
	1 person in cabin	£35.00
2-bedded de-luxe cabin	2 persons in cabin	£21.00
	1 person in cabin	£35.00

NOTE: outside de-luxe cabins have portholes, inside de-luxe cabins and all economy cabins have no portholes.
All de-luxe cabins have shower, wash basin and w.c.

10   One-sided dialogue: at a restaurant

Read the following dialogue with Student B.

Unfortunately, you can only see your part, so you will have to listen very carefully to what Student B says. Use the menu on the next page.

Before starting, read through your part to get an idea of what the dialogue is all about.

You:	It's a nice restaurant, don't you think?
Student B:	......
You:	No, not really. What about you?
Student B:	......
You:	Oh, I see. Now, let's have a look at the menu. (*slight pause*) What would you like to start with?
Student B:	......
You:	Yes, I think I'll have the same. No, on second thoughts, I'll have...... (*name a dish*).
Student B:	......
You:	Well, I don't like...... (*repeat dish*) very much, actually. I think I'd prefer...... (*name another dish*). I had it the last time I was here and it was really delicious.
Student B:	......
You:	Yes, good. And what about some vegetables with the meal?
Student B:	......
You:	Yes, let's see. (*slight pause*) I think I'll have...... (*name two vegetables*).
Student B:	......
You:	Right. Now, where's the waiter?

THE INN PLACE

TABLE D'HOTE DINNER MENU

£6.95

Iced Melon	Grapefruit Cocktail
Avocado Pear	Pâté Maison
Prawn Cocktail	Various Soups

Grilled Halibut with Lemon
Baked Plaice and Mushrooms
Veal Escalope
Minute Steak Garni
Lamb and Mushroom Ragoût
Roast Turkey with Rosemary Butter Stuffing
Chicken and Bacon Pie
Rice and Mushroom Salad
Cold Meat Salads (Various)

Chips	Soufflé Potatoes	Garden Peas
New Potatoes	Carrots	French Beans
Tomatoes	Mushrooms	Cauliflower

Fruit Salad	Various Ice Creams
Apple Pie	Cheese and Biscuits

Coffee and Drinks Extra

Service Charge Included

11   Looking for a house/flat (1)

You have a farmhouse to let in North Wales. The address is 'Mountain Farm', Bala. It is near Lake Bala and sleeps five people comfortably. It is quite modern and has, among other things, a colour T.V. and a dish-washer. It is surrounded by beautiful countryside and is ideal for fishing, walking among the mountains, etc. It is available from 1 July to 28 September and costs £80 a week during July and August and £70 a week during September.

You have put an advertisement in the newspaper about it. Student B is going to phone you up for further details.

12   Looking for a house/flat (2)

HOUSES, FLATS, etc.
Various properties to be let

House on South coast to let. 3 weeks in July or August.
Phone: Hastings 123750

Large flat in Chelsea available now.
Phone: 01-101 3267 (after 6 p.m.)

You are an architect and are moving to London at the end of August. You are looking for a flat – preferably near Chelsea or Kensington. You want a modern flat (especially the kitchen and bathroom) with more than one bedroom and with a garage if possible. You are prepared to pay up to £50 a week.

You see the advertisement on the previous page in the newspaper and decide to phone up about it. Student B owns the flat.

You can begin like this:

Good (*evening*). I'm phoning about the flat.

(Note: If you are interested in the flat after your telephone conversation, arrange a time to go and see it.)

13   Fill in the missing information (1)

By asking Student B questions, fill in the missing information in the table on the next page. (Student B will also ask you questions.)
Before starting, work out the type of questions you will need to ask. For example:

Who is arriving on ... (*say date*)?
What nationality is ... (*say name*)?
When is ... (*say name*) ... arriving at the conference?
How long is ... (*say name*) ... staying?
At which hotel is ... (*say name*) ... staying?
At what time is ... (*say name*) ... giving a lecture?
On what date is the lecture on ... (*say subject*)?
etc.

When you have both finished, compare your tables to check that you have filled in the missing information correctly.

(Note: If, in answer to one of your questions, Student B says he/she doesn't know the answer, then try another sort of question to get the same information, since it may be that Student B has not yet filled in the information you based your first question on.)

INTERNATIONAL CONFERENCE ON PSYCHIC RESEARCH

London, 6 June–20 June

List and details of participants

	Name	Nationality	Date of arrival	Length of stay	Hotel
1		American	5 June		The Hilton
2	Sven Borg			10 days	Central Park
3	Dr Marina Rossi	Italian	7 June	4 days	The Dorchester
4			6 June	a week	Royal Kensington
5	Dr Klaus von Braun	German	10 June	5 days	The Dorchester
6	Sir Roger Bloom	English		2 weeks	Cen
7	Viktor Pavlova	Russian	3 June		

	Date and time of lecture		Subject of lecture
1	10 June	2.30 p.m.	In Search of UFOs
2	8 June	9.30 a.m.	The Secret of Dreams
3	9 June	3.15 p.m.	
4	11 June	10 a.m.	Psychic Healing
5	12 June		
6		10.15 a.m.	The Secret Life of Plants
7	15 June		The Great Tele

14 Questionnaire: children and parents

Read through the sentences below then put a circle around the number which most closely coincides with your opinion. Before starting, look at the Key.

KEY	
1	Yes, definitely
2	Yes, perhaps
3	Well, that depends
4	No, not really
5	No, definitely not

Children should obey their parents without question.	1 2 3 4 5
It is an advantage to be an only child.	1 2 3 4 5
Girls and boys should be brought up in the same way – without definite roles.	1 2 3 4 5
Most men would prefer to have a son as their first child.	1 2 3 4 5
You should never hit a child.	1 2 3 4 5
It is a child's duty to look after his or her parents when they are old.	1 2 3 4 5
Parents should never quarrel in front of their children.	1 2 3 4 5
The best way of punishing a child is to stop his or her pocket money.	1 2 3 4 5
Babies are boring.	1 2 3 4 5
It is wrong for both parents to go out to work if they have small children.	1 2 3 4 5
No family should be allowed to have more than four children nowadays.	1 2 3 4 5
Children under 18 should never be out later than 11 o'clock in the evening.	1 2 3 4 5

When you have finished, discuss your answers with Student B.
Remember to give reasons for your opinion – and even to argue with what Student B says if you disagree with him or her.

Complete the drawing (1)

Student B has an incomplete map of Black Island.

Help him/her to complete it by telling him/her what to draw and answering his/her questions. But you must not touch his/her map or let him/her see yours.

When you have finished, compare maps.

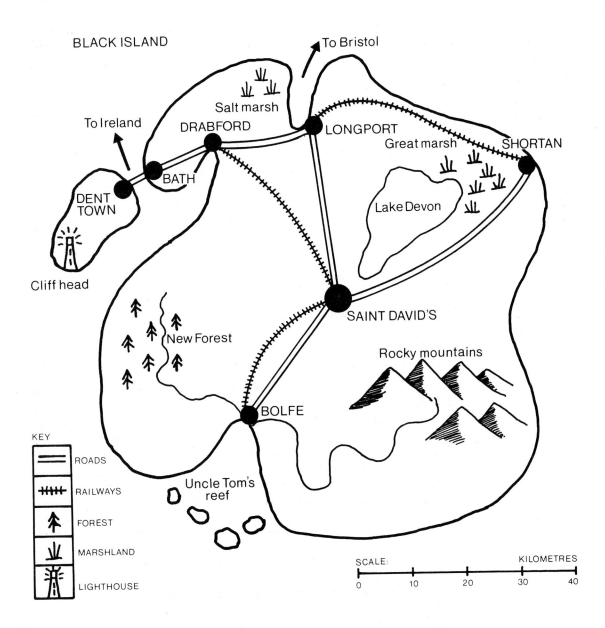

16   Complete the drawing (2)

Below is an incomplete weather map of Great Britain. Student B has a completed version. He/she is going to help you complete yours.

You are allowed to ask questions but you must not look at Student B's map.

When you have finished, compare your drawings.

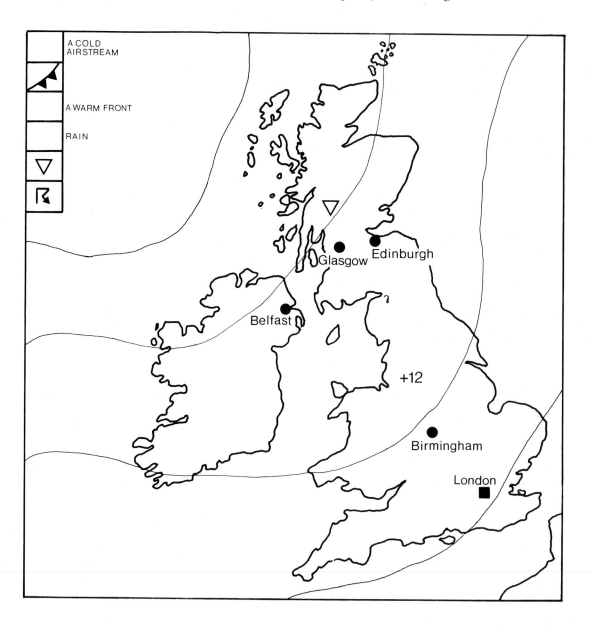

A COLD AIRSTREAM

A WARM FRONT

RAIN

Glasgow
Edinburgh
Belfast
+12
Birmingham
London

Newspaper interviews (1) 17

You write the gossip column for the *Daily Mirror*. You are going to interview Albert Sykes/Anita Sykes, the gardener who recently got married to his/her employer – the famous detective-story writer, Anthea Crystal/Arthur Crystal.

Student B is Albert Sykes/Anita Sykes.

Before starting, work out some questions to ask. For example:

> When did you start working for Miss/Mr Crystal?
> What was she/he like to work for?
> What was she/he like as a person?
> When did your romance start? How?
> Where did you go for your honeymoon? Why?
> etc.

You can begin like this:

> How do you do, Mr Sykes/Mrs Crystal. I'm (*David Brown*) of the *Daily Mirror*. It was kind of you to let me interview you.

Newspaper interviews (2)

Your name is Antonio Arpeggio/Antonia Arpeggio.

You are a film director. Last week, your film *Lucky* won no less than five Oscars, including the 'Best picture of the year' and the 'Best director' awards. The film, written by you, only cost $300,000 to make and is the story of a poor black boy called Lucky Leroy who rises from the slums of New York to become President of the U.S.A.

You wrote the film over seven years ago but it took a long time to get the money to make it. (None of the major film companies were interested. They called it 'rubbish'.)

You thought it was a good film but are surprised at how well it has gone down with the public. So far the film has made over $1 million. You think people like it because it has very little violence and is the story of the 'little man' making good – the old 'American dream'.

You have agreed to be interviewed by a reporter from the magazine *The Cinema Today*. Student B is the reporter.

When you answer his/her questions, try to use your own words as much as possible.

Questionnaire: opinions and attitudes

Read through the sentences below, then put a circle around the number which most closely coincides with your opinion. Before starting, look at the Key.

There is no life after death.	1 2 3 4 5	**KEY**
Wars never solve anything.	1 2 3 4 5	1 I agree entirely
We should try to cure criminals, not punish them.	1 2 3 4 5	2 I agree on the whole
People suffering from incurable diseases should be painlessly put to death if they request it.	1 2 3 4 5	3 I can't make up my mind
Men and women can never be equal.	1 2 3 4 5	4 I disagree on the whole
It is wrong to pay people so much money for playing sport.	1 2 3 4 5	5 I disagree entirely
People should wait until they are at least 24 before getting married.	1 2 3 4 5	
People were a lot happier 'in the old days'.	1 2 3 4 5	
There is too much fuss made about nuclear power nowadays.	1 2 3 4 5	
Divorce is wrong.	1 2 3 4 5	
Most people keep pets because they are lonely or have difficulty in making relationships with other people.	1 2 3 4 5	
The United Nations is a waste of time and money.	1 2 3 4 5	

When you have finished, discuss your answers with Student B. Remember to give reasons for your opinion – and even to argue with Student B if you disagree with him or her.

You are a foreign student and have been invited to Horam Primary School for the day. You have just gone into this classroom. Student B is the class teacher and you are going to ask him/her questions about the school and the children. For instance:

> What sort of school is it?
> How many children are there in the school?
> How old are the children in this class?
> What lesson are you doing at the moment?
> What time do they start and finish school?
> Are they interested in learning?
> etc.

Look at the photograph and try to ask other questions. (You may even want to ask about some of the children in the photograph.)

When you have finished, you can say:

> Thank you very much for letting me see the school. It's been really interesting.

Visiting a factory

You are the Works Manager at Clothewell Limited – a firm which makes women's clothing. You are showing a foreign student (Student B) around and have just taken him to this part of the factory. He/she is going to ask you questions about the factory and the people who work there.

Before starting, think about the following:

> What the factory makes
> What is going on in the photograph
> Number of employees (men or women)
> When they start/finish work (shift-work)
> How much the people in the photograph earn
> If you export – where
> What sort of clothes are most/least popular
> etc.

(Note: If you don't know the true answers to Student B's questions, use your imagination!)

22 One-sided dialogue: what shall we do this weekend?

Read the following dialogue with Student B.

You are friends and are talking about where to go at the weekend.

Unfortunately, you can only see your part of the dialogue, so you will have to listen very carefully to what Student B says. Use the *Weekend Guide* on the opposite page.

Before starting, read through your part to get an idea of what the dialogue is all about.

Student B: ......
You: What do you mean?
Student B: ......
You: Yes, all right. What do you suggest?
Student B: ......
You: Well, why not look in tonight's paper? There's usually a *Weekend Guide* on Thursdays.
Student B: ......
You: What?
Student B: ......
You: No, ... (*give reason why you don't like the suggestion*).
Student B: ......
You: Well, that's an idea, I suppose, but I'm not all that keen, really.
Student B: ......
You: Er ... what about ...... (*suggest something from EXHIBI-TIONS*).
Student B: ......
You: All right. It was only a suggestion (*slight pause*). Of course, we could always ...... (*make a suggestion from SPORTING EVENTS*).
Student B: ......
You: ...... (*read out the information*).
Student B: ......
You: Yes, that's fine by me.
Student B: ......

WEEKEND GUIDE

EXHIBITIONS

Women at War, 1914-1918
Photographic record. Public Library. Saturday 10–6.

Costumes Through the Ages
Costumes from the 16th century to today. Local Museum. Sat–Mon 10–4.30.

Model Railway Exhibition
Goldenhill Model Railway Club, St Andrew's Hall. Saturday 11–7. At least 16 working layouts on view.

SPORTING EVENTS

Tenpin Bowling
National Championships at The Bowl. All day Saturday and Sunday.

Charity Football Match
Charity football match between House of Commons team and Entertainers team at Pilot Fields. Saturday afternoon 2 p.m.

Stockcar Racing
International meeting at Burlight. Disco afterwards. Saturday afternoon 2.15 p.m.

COACH TOURS

Castle Howard, York
The most beautiful historic house in Yorkshire. Grounds, restaurant and cafeteria. House and Costume Gallery. Depart Saturday 8.30 a.m.

Kent Coastal Tour
See pleasant countryside of Kent as well as miles of coastline. Lunch at Dover. Depart Saturday 10 a.m.

Mystery Tour
Tour to somewhere famous. Details will not be given until you arrive. Depart Saturday 9 a.m.

OTHER EVENTS

Special Weekend for Railway Enthusiasts
Photographic weekend with special events including a 'Steam up' at Dackton Transport Museum. Saturday and Sunday 11 a.m.–5.30 p.m.

Antiques Fair
Opens on Saturday at Old Town Arts Centre. Saturday 11.30 a.m.–7.30 p.m. Admission £1.

Flower Power
Daffodil Festival at Otram. Two tons of bulbs already planted and a further 10,000 will decorate village. Saturday and Sunday.

Chess Championships
National chess championships on the Pier. Saturday–Tuesday 10.30 a.m.–7.30 p.m.

Asking for and giving directions

Take it in turns with Student B to ask for and give directions using the street plan on the opposite page.

You want directions for the following places (in this order):

FROM	TO
1 the station	the police station
2 the police station	the boutique
3 the boutique	the post office
4 the post office	the museum
5 the museum	the restaurant

When Student B gives you directions, write the name (e.g. Police Station) on the appropriate building.

The names of the buildings on the street plan opposite are the places Student B wants directions to. He/she is going to ask directions for the following places (in this order):

FROM	TO
1 the station	the bank
2 the bank	the book shop
3 the book shop	the Grand Hotel
4 the Grand Hotel	the drugstore
5 the drugstore	the coffee bar

Ask for and give directions alternately. You start. When you ask for directions, you can say:

Excuse me,	could you tell me the way to can you tell me how to get to	(*the museum*),	please?

When you have finished, compare street plans to check that you have written the names of the various buildings in the correct places.

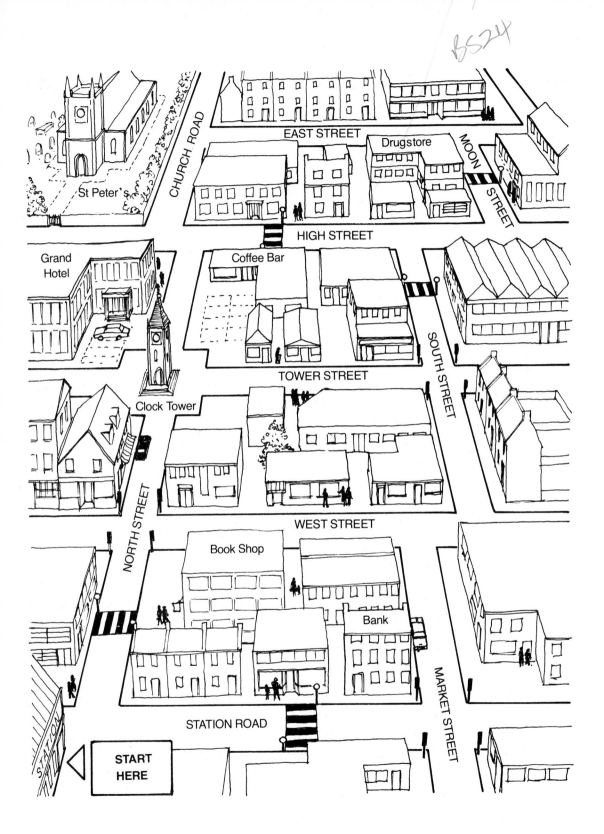

BS24

St Peter's

CHURCH ROAD

EAST STREET

Drugstore

MOON STREET

HIGH STREET

Grand Hotel

Coffee Bar

SOUTH STREET

TOWER STREET

Clock Tower

NORTH STREET

WEST STREET

Book Shop

Bank

MARKET STREET

STATION ROAD

START HERE

41

Complete the drawing (3)

Below is a plan of a flat with the furniture missing. Student B has the same plan but with the furniture put in. He/she is going to help you furnish your flat by telling you what to draw and where to put it. (A guide is given to the various items of furniture.)

You are allowed to ask questions but you must not look at Student B's drawing. When you have finished, compare drawings.

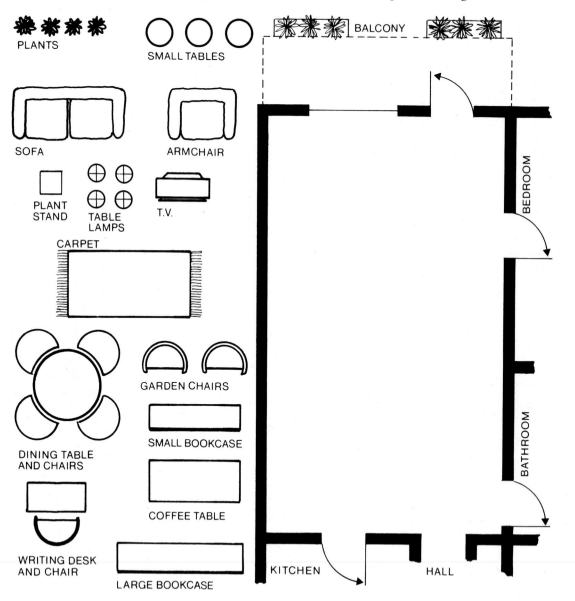

PLANTS

SMALL TABLES

BALCONY

SOFA

ARMCHAIR

PLANT STAND

TABLE LAMPS

T.V.

CARPET

BEDROOM

GARDEN CHAIRS

DINING TABLE AND CHAIRS

SMALL BOOKCASE

BATHROOM

COFFEE TABLE

WRITING DESK AND CHAIR

LARGE BOOKCASE

KITCHEN

HALL

Complete the drawing (4)

Below is a drawing of a kitchen with pots, glasses, etc. Student B has the same drawing but without any of the pots, glasses, etc. Help him/her place the various objects by telling him/her where to put them. (A guide to the objects is given below.)

Student B can ask questions but he/she must not see your drawing. When you have finished, compare your drawings.

TEAPOT   GLASSES   LOAF   BREAD KNIFE   CUPS AND SAUCERS

COFFEE   CUPS

TEA   PLATES   SAUCEPAN   WASHING POWDER

VASE OF FLOWERS   CANDLE   BUCKET   PLANT   BOTTLES   BRUSH

Below are four situations which you are going to act out with Student B. Before starting, read through the situations (especially number 2 and number 4) and think a little about what you will say.

When you are both ready, act out the situation.

Situation 1

You are sitting at home reading through a holiday brochure about Spain. You have decided to go there on holiday next summer with a friend and are looking forward to it very much. Suddenly, the phone rings. It is the friend you are going on holiday with. You are glad he or she has phoned because you would like to ask him or her one or two questions about your summer plans.

Situation 2

You are due to get married next month. Last Saturday you went to a party (without your fiancé or fiancée) and met someone else. You fell in love with him or her immediately and, as a result, you no longer feel you can go through with the marriage. You decide to phone up your fiancé or fiancée to try to explain in as nice a way as possible why the marriage is off.

Situation 3

You have been quarrelling with your neighbour about his dog which is always coming into your garden. You have just had another row and have come into the house to try to cool down when there is a knock at the door. You think it is your neighbour and fling the door open – ready to carry on the argument. But you find yourself face-to-face with a complete stranger.

Situation 4

You have been to a concert in a town fifteen kilometres away from your home. Unfortunately, you have missed the last bus home and also find that you do not have enough money for a taxi. However, you remember the name and address of a friend of your brother's and decide to go and ask him or her if he or she can help you. You arrive at the house and knock at the door.

Fill in the missing information (2)

By asking Student B questions, fill in the missing information in the Immigrant Survey Sheet below in pencil. (Student B will also ask you questions.)

IMMIGRANT SURVEY SHEET   July 19

Name: ....Abraham Jacobs.......   Nationality: ....

Occupation: ...Bus driver.........   Married/Single

Number of children: ....

Length of time in Britain: ......– years................................

Date of arrival: ....June 17th 1970....................................

Reason for coming to Britain: ....

....

Present address (town/village only): ...Birmingham........

Length of time in present town/village: ....

Other towns/villages where person has lived: ...London....

...Bradford, Liverpool..

Knowledge of English:

1 on arrival: Good/quite good/fairly good/poor

2 now: Good/quite good/fairly good/poor

Number of English courses attended: ....

Language(s) spoken at home: ....

Problems/difficulties living in Britain:

1 ...Difficult to get a good job..

2 ...Difficult to find decent accommodation............................

3 ...Colour prejudice..

4 ...Not considered to be English......................................

Contact with English people:

1 at work: ....

2 outside work: ....

When you have finished, compare books to check that you have filled in the missing information correctly.

Meeting an old friend

You are Roger (or Joanna) Morgan.

You meet an old friend, Claire (or Peter) Smith, on the Underground whom you haven't seen since he/she got married ten years ago. (You went abroad a few days after the wedding.) You used to go to school with her husband, Bill/his wife, Rita, who used to dance well and whose father owned an antique shop. The last you heard, they were emigrating to Canada.

When you last saw him/her you were going out with Alison (Alistair) who is Scottish. Have a chat and arrange to meet again in the near future.

Before starting, read through the above so that you remember the details without having to look at them too closely. Also think about what has happened to you since you last met (e.g. Are you married? What's your job? Where are you living? etc.).

When you are ready, you can begin. Here are some phrases you can use:

(a)	the meeting:	Good heavens! It's (*Claire*), isn't it?
(b)	talking about appearance:	You look different. What is it? You've changed. (*You're much fatter*), etc.
(c)	asking questions:	How's..... (*Bill*)? Where are you living/working nowadays? Do you still..... (*go dancing*)? Didn't you go to Canada? etc.
(d)	taking leave:	I must go now, I'm afraid. I've got to.....
(e)	making arrangements:	We must meet again some time.

Above all, be prepared to use your imagination!
Student B is Claire Smith or Peter Smith.
Note that *Alison* is a Scottish girl's name.

29   After the holiday

Think of somewhere in your country that would be an ideal place to go on holiday. Now imagine that you are English and have just spent two weeks in this place. You are travelling home by bus from London when you get into conversation with the person sitting next to you (Student B), and end up talking about your holiday.

Before starting, think about the following:

> - where you went
> - why you chose this place for a holiday
> - how you travelled
> - who you went with
> - where you stayed
> - how you spent your time
> - who you met
> - what sort of food you ate
> - what the weather was like
> - what souvenirs you bought
> - how much the holiday cost altogether
> - if you would recommend it to someone else
>   etc.

When you are both ready, you can start. Student B begins.

Questionnaire: the future

Read through the sentences below, each of which deals with an event in the future, and put a circle around the number which most closely coincides with your opinion. Before starting, look at the Key.

		KEY
I will get married.	1 2 3 4 5 6 7	
Solar energy will replace oil.	1 2 3 4 5 6 7	1 Yes, definitely
There will be a major accident at a nuclear power station.	1 2 3 4 5 6 7	2 Yes, probably 3 It's possible 4 It's impossible to say
I will move to and work in a foreign country for a while.	1 2 3 4 5 6 7	5 It's doubtful 6 No, probably not 7 No, definitely not
Cities will be built in Antarctica.	1 2 3 4 5 6 7	
A UFO or flying saucer will land near a large city.	1 2 3 4 5 6 7	
I will have at least two children.	1 2 3 4 5 6 7	
Whales will become extinct.	1 2 3 4 5 6 7	
Britain will have a president instead of a king or queen.	1 2 3 4 5 6 7	
I will be able to speak English fluently.	1 2 3 4 5 6 7	
There will be a female President of the U.S.A.	1 2 3 4 5 6 7	
I will keep in touch with the people in my present English class (by writing, etc.).	1 2 3 4 5 6 7	

When you have finished, discuss your answers with Student B. Try to give reasons for your certainty or uncertainty as well as asking Student B why he/she is so certain/uncertain something will or will not happen.

31   Looking for a job (1)

Situations Vacant

Music business family require
NANNY/MOTHER'S HELP.
Over 20. Not far from London.
Phone: Bucks 2176

Looking for a job this summer?
TUTOR required for 10-year-old
Jonathan during 6-week yacht
cruise among Greek islands.
Phone: 01-333 8739

You teach a class of 11-year-olds at a primary school in Brighton. You have had this job for three years. You are looking for a summer job to help buy a new car in the autumn. You do not mind what sort of job it is, but possibly teaching foreign students or looking after children would do.

You are prepared to work in any part of the country or even abroad. You would hope to earn at least £80 a week and are available from 20 July until 8 September.

You see the above advertisement in the newspaper and decide to phone up about it. Student B is Jonathan's mother/father.

You can begin like this:

Good (*afternoon*). I'm phoning about the advertisement in today's paper.

Looking for a job (2)

You are looking for a regular baby-sitter for your two children – Andrew, aged 7, and Constance, aged 5. It would be every Saturday evening from 7 p.m. until about 12.30–1 a.m.

You are looking for a girl or boy between 16 and 18 (preferably still at school). You would prefer someone with experience and, if possible, references.

You will either pick the person up and run him/her home or arrange for a taxi for him/her. You do not want to pay more than £1 a night since you will also be providing food. You have a very large house. Your address is 213 Lansington High Street.

You have put an advertisement in the newspaper for a baby-sitter. Student B phones up about it. If you think he/she sounds suitable, arrange a time to see him/her – preferably after 6 p.m.

33   Asking for information about a town

You are a clerk at the Tourist and Recreation Office in Hastings. Student B phones you up for information about the town. Answer his/her questions with the help of the information sheet below. (Read through it before starting.)

Population:	75,000.
Climate:	Mild and sunny. Low rainfall. 2,000 hours sunshine last year.
Sights:	Long promenade (five kilometres), pier, Old Town, castle, parks and gardens, caves, model village, miniature railway, Hastings Embroidery.
Entertainment:	Two cinemas, two theatres, concerts, discotheques, pubs, Leisure Centre, bingo, cricket, children's playground.
Sports:	Golf, putting, bowls, fishing, tennis, swimming, squash.
Communications:	90 mins from London by rail. 99 kilometres by road through some of the loveliest countryside in South-East England.
Accommodation:	Hotels, guest houses, holiday flats, caravans.
Restaurants:	Italian, Chinese, Indian. In Old Town lots of fish and chip shops.

Some places of interest	Battle Abbey (9 kilometres) Bodiam Castle (17 kilometres) Pevensey Castle (19 kilometres) Old towns of Winchelsea and Rye (14 and 17 kilometres)

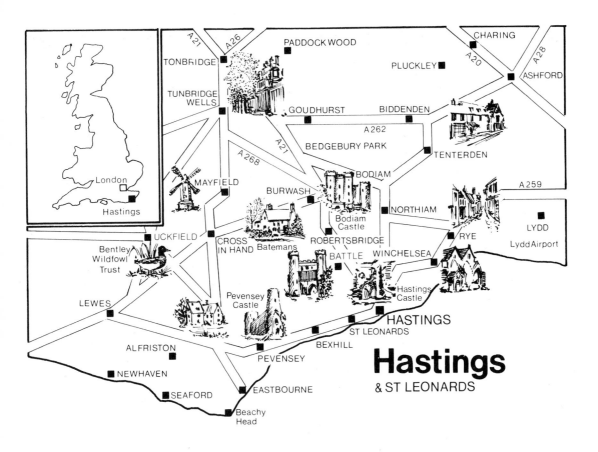

CHARING

TONBRIDGE

A21 A26

PADDOCK WOOD

PLUCKLEY

A20

A28

ASHFORD

TUNBRIDGE WELLS

GOUDHURST

BIDDENDEN

A262

BEDGEBURY PARK

TENTERDEN

MAYFIELD

A268

A21

BODIAM

A259

BURWASH

Bodiam Castle

NORTHIAM

RYE

LYDD

Lydd Airport

UCKFIELD

CROSS IN HAND

Batemans

ROBERTSBRIDGE

BATTLE

WINCHELSEA

Bentley Wildfowl Trust

Hastings Castle

LEWES

Pevensey Castle

HASTINGS

ST LEONARDS

ALFRISTON

PEVENSEY

BEXHILL

Hastings
& ST LEONARDS

NEWHAVEN

SEAFORD

EASTBOURNE

Beachy Head

London

Hastings

34 Asking for information about summer language courses

You are thinking of sending your son or daughter to England in the summer on a language course. You phone up Summer Language Courses (an organization which arranges such courses) for further details.

Student B works for Summer Language Courses.

Before starting, work out the type of information you require and the sort of questions you are going to ask. For example:

–	centres	In which towns do you have summer courses?
–	course length	How long do the courses last?
–	accommodation	Will my son/daughter stay with an English family, or what?
–	tuition	How many hours a day teaching will he/she get?
–	cost etc.	How much does it cost?

When you are ready, you can begin like this:

> Good (*afternoon*). I'm thinking of sending my (*son*) to England in the summer on a language course. I wonder if you could tell me something about the courses you run?

THE
ENGLISH
INSTITUTE

Make this the year you learn English.
'Special' courses starting next week:

Business English ∗ Medical English
Banking English ∗ Tourist English
Cambridge First Certificate
Cambridge Proficiency
Looking at Britain

For further details, phone 767 56342

You are a foreign student living in Britain. You are interested in one of these courses. You phone up The English Institute for further details about the course. Student B is a secretary at The English Institute.

Before starting, have a pen ready to make a note of the following:

Course number: ....

Day/Days: ....

Time: ....

Length of course: .... weeks

Number of meetings: ....

Length of each meeting: .... hours

Cost: £ ....

Name of teacher: ....

You can begin like this:

Good (*afternoon*). I'd like to enrol for one of the courses starting next week.

36
One-sided dialogue: arranging an interview with 'Rubber'

Read the following dialogue with Student B.

You are 'Sticky' Hansen, the manager of the famous Swedish pop group, RUBBER. You are on tour in England and are staying at a hotel in London. A magazine reporter phones you up to try to arrange an interview with the group. Student B is the reporter.

Unfortunately, you can only see your part of the dialogue, so you will have to listen very carefully to what Student B says. Use the diary on the page opposite.

Before starting, read through your part to get an idea of what the dialogue is all about.

You:	...... (*say your name*).
Student B:	......
You:	Next week? Er ... what day did you have in mind?
Student B:	......
You:	...... (*repeat day*)? What time?
Student B:	......
You:	...... (*repeat time*). Well, if you'd hold on a minute, Mr/Miss...... (*say name*), I'll just check through the group's diary for next week.
Student B:	......
	(*You look at the diary.*)
You:	Hello?
Student B:	......
You:	No, I'm afraid......'s (*say day*) impossible. ...... (*explain why and suggest Tuesday morning instead*).
Student B:	......
You:	Well, what days would suit you, then?
Student B:	......
You:	...... (*repeat day and look at diary*). Yes, that would be all right with us. But what time exactly?
Student B:	......
You:	...... (*repeat time and write it down*). And your name was......?
Student B:	......
You:	Right, Mr/Miss...... (*say name*). I'll let RUBBER know when I see them this afternoon. You'll come to the hotel, I presume?
Student B:	......
You:	Yes, of course.
Student B:	......
You:	Thank you. Good-bye.

morning	afternoon	
Photo session with RUBBER 9.30		**5** Monday

morning	afternoon	
	Recording session 1.30	**6** Tuesday

morning	afternoon	
RUBBER to B.B.C. T.V. show 10 — Drive to Wales	to record 4.30 in the evening	**7** Wednesday

morning	afternoon	
RUBBER to open new bridge in Wales 11.15	Drive back to London	**8** Thursday

morning	afternoon	
	Leave for Scotland 1.30	**9** Friday

You work for Sunshine Touring. As a result of last-minute cancellations you are offering a number of holidays at reduced rates. Student B phones you up about one of them. Give him/her all the necessary information with the help of the holiday information on the opposite page.

Then, if he/she is interested in booking a holiday, fill in the holiday booking form.

SUNSHINE TOURING   Holiday Booking Form

Number of days: ....

Destination

Departure

Day	Time	Flight No.

Name: ....

Address: ....

....

Tel. No.: ....

SUNSHINE TOURING

PLACE	DAY	TIME	FLIGHT NO.	NO. OF DAYS	HOTEL	PRICE
Majorca	Sat	13.30	BE 237	14	Santa Lucia	£96
Athens	Tues	09.30	OA 142	10	Rivoli	£75
Crete	Sun	19.30	BE 672	14	El Greco	£120
Paris	Sun	16.00	AF 924	7	Normandie	£55
Rome	Mon	08.15	BE 312	10	Londra	£100
Rhodes	Sat	18.00	LH 007	14	Carina	£150
Barcelona	Tues	16.20	BE 172	10	Do Carmo	£80
Oslo	Sat	19.30	SA 895	7	Sheraton	£100

By asking Student B questions, fill in the missing information in the letter of application below. (Student B will also ask you questions.)

Tel: ....   10, Grove Road,
                                                       Bristol

Personnel Manager,
G. Hoover & Co.,
Linton Estate,
Manchester   14th January, 19..

Dear Sir,

I should like to apply for the post of Export Manager which I saw
advertised in last Saturday's Daily Chronicle.

I am ..... years old and unmarried.   At present I am Assistant
Manager at Wright & Company, a firm which makes reproduction
furniture, much of which is sold for export to France and Germany.
Prior to this, I worked for .... years as a secretary at I.B.M.
and three years as ....

I attended .... School from the age of
eleven to eighteen, where I obtained ..... O-levels and ..... A-level.
After this I went on to Brighton College of Further Education, where
I obtained ....   At present
I am attending courses in .... and .... and have a working
knowledge of both languages.

Although I enjoy my present job, I should like one which offers more
responsibility and especially a job where I would be able to use my
own initiative and travel abroad.   My present salary is ....

I enclose my present employer's name as referee and look forward to
hearing from you.

Yours faithfully,

Julie Evans

When you have finished, compare books to check that you have filled
in the missing information correctly.

Note to teacher on optional activities

The following two activities are included as *optional* extras rather than forming part of the main book since it was felt that they would not be appropriate for all students. Basically, these activities are examples of what can be termed 'oral jigsaw reading'; that is, where a text, a dialogue, etc. has been cut up and rearranged out of sequence. Each student is then given half the pieces and by working together they try to re-form the whole. But they must do this orally; they are not allowed to show one another their pieces of the text, dialogue, etc.

This is a very useful language activity since it not only tests the students' comprehension but is also a useful communicative activity which practises a number of language functions. For example:

asking for things to be repeated. (Could you read that bit again, please?)
agreeing/disagreeing. (No, I don't think that goes next./Yes, that goes next.)
suggesting. (Why don't you read out the bits you have left?/Let's read it through again from the beginning, shall we?)
making logical deductions. (This must be the next bit./That can't come next. There's something missing.)
etc.

Teaching hints

1. As in all the other activities in the book students work in pairs facing one another with some sort of screen between them to avoid seeing one another's books.

2. Since the instructions for the two activities are the same in both students' books, the teacher should make sure that the students understand what they have to do by going through the instructions with the whole class before the students begin the activity.

3. Once the students understand what they should do, the teacher should leave them to do it and should at all costs avoid the temptation to step in and offer help or suggestions on how to solve the problem.

4. Once everyone has finished, the teacher can check that the activity has been completed correctly by asking one pair to read out the text, dialogue, etc. in sequence.

5. It is often worth having a short discussion about each activity afterwards to find out what the students found difficult and in particular to see whether there was anything they wished to say but did not know how to say it.

39   Sort it out: two letters

The following jumbled-up pieces of writing are from two letters. Unfortunately, you have only got half the pieces. Student B has the other half. Working together, try to sort out both letters. You must not show your pieces to Student B, but you can read them out. Student B begins. Together, mark the first letter 1–6 and the second one a–h. When you have finished, check by reading the letters out loud. (The first bit of one letter is marked.)

stop now as there's a football match starting on TV in a few minutes. But do write and tell us when your plane arrives so we can pick you up at the airport.

also a surprise to hear that Mrs Jones has moved to Scotland. Have you got any new neighbours yet?
About this summer – yes, I am thinking of coming to Torquay again, and one of my chief reasons for writing

Peter and the cats!
Looking forward to hearing from you soon.

Lots of love,
Anna

P.S. My parents send you their regards.

when your plane arrives at Gatwick we can come and pick you up in the car. We might even arrange to have Peter with us! (He keeps asking about you every time we see him.)

a

Dear Anna,
How nice to hear from you and to learn that you are thinking of returning to Torquay this summer. Of course you can stay with us – we'd love to have you. In fact, Jan was saying only the other day how nice

time for the Carnival!) Or is it at a different time this year? Anyway, it doesn't really matter because there are so many other things to look forward to in England.

so we've ended up keeping them! You'll meet them when you come here.
What else was there? Oh yes! The Carnival is on 20 July, so you'll be in time for it again. As for

40   **Sort it out: a dialogue**

The following jumbled-up sentences are from a dialogue where a Mr/Mrs Simpson, an American artist, is met at an Underground station in London by a Mr/Miss Jenkins, who works for a gallery where Mr/Mrs Simpson is having an exhibition. Unfortunately, you have only got Mr/Miss Jenkins's part. Student B has Mr/Mrs Simpson's part. Working together, try to sort out the dialogue. You must not show your part to Student B, but you can read out the sentences. Together, mark the dialogue 1–16. (Your part will be marked 1, 3, 5 etc.)

When you have finished, check by reading the dialogue out loud. You say the first speech in the dialogue and it is marked.

Right, Viv. This way then.

Yes, I'm afraid so. You had a pleasant flight, I hope?

I'm so pleased to meet you. I'm Pat Jenkins from the Soho Gallery. How do you do.

Well, I'm afraid I don't know. I've never flown in anything faster than a DC 10.

Yes, I'm sure it is. Well, Mr/Mrs Simpson, perhaps you'd care to come this way. We can take a taxi to the Gallery.

---

1.   Excuse me, but it is Mr/Mrs Simpson, isn't it?

The Concorde? Yes, it is, rather. It was your first supersonic flight, was it, Mr/Mrs Simpson?

Not at all. I know how difficult it can be to find your way about in a strange city.